LATIMER STUDY 80

WERE THEY
PREACHING
'ANOTHER GOSPEL'?

Justification by Faith in the Second Century

D1565354

BY ANDREW DAUNTON-FEAR

The Latimer Trust

BT
764.3
.D38
2015

Were They Preaching 'Another Gospel'? Justification by Faith in the Second Century © Andrew Daunton-Fear 2015 All rights reserved.

ISBN 978-1-906327-30-9

Cover photo: Cave church in Ihlara valley, Turkey© mathess – fotolia.com

Scripture quotations are from New Revised Standard Version Bible, copyright © 1989 National Council of the Churches of Christ in the United States of America. Used by permission. All rights reserved.

Published by the Latimer Trust March 2015

The Latimer Trust (formerly Latimer House, Oxford) is a conservative Evangelical research organisation within the Church of England, whose main aim is to promote the history and theology of Anglicanism as understood by those in the Reformed tradition. Interested readers are welcome to consult its website for further details of its many activities.

The Latimer Trust
London N14 4PS UK
Registered Charity: 1084337
Company Number: 4104465
Web: www.latimertrust.org
E-mail: administrator@latimertrust.org

Views expressed in works published by The Latimer Trust are those of the authors and do not necessarily represent the official position of The Latimer Trust.

CONTENTS

Foreword

I recommend this booklet, a fresh look at the theme of justification by faith in the Early Church. It is always helpful to test and examine the truthfulness of common assumptions, and Andrew encourages us to see that Paul's teaching on justification by faith was present in the writings of Early Church leaders. He does not claim that it had the prominence or detailed and applied expression that it had at the Reformation: it would be unrealistic to expect that to be the case. However the evidence that Andrew provides gives us a useful insight into the Early Church, and its perception and use of this key Pauline and Biblical doctrine.

Peter Adam,
Vicar-Emeritus of St. Jude's Carlton, Melbourne,
Formerly Principal of Ridley College.

Acknowledgements

I would like to express deep gratitude to the Executive Committee of the Latimer Trust for kindly accepting this paper for publication as a Latimer Study; also to the Rev. Dr. Peter Adam, once a student of mine at Ridley College, Melbourne, later for ten years Principal of that institution. Warm thanks too to the Very Rev. Dr. Gloria Mapangdol, Dean and President of St. Andrew's Theological Seminary, Manila, for drawing my attention to the articles by George Howard and Arland J. Hultgren referred to in the New Testament section of this paper; also to Greg Bradshaw of Ortigas, Manila, and Helmut Wilhelm of Lichtenberg, Berlin, for valuable assistance with German translation. Finally many thanks to my dear wife Jennifer for tolerating being shut out of my study during the many hours of preparation of my script!

Andrew Daunton-Fear

About the Author

Andrew Daunton-Fear studied theology at Cambridge, where he gained a love of the Early Church from his teacher, the prolific author William Frend. He was then invited by Principal Leon Morris to assist with teaching New Testament and Church History at Ridley College, Melbourne. While in Australia he was ordained at St. Paul's Cathedral, Melbourne.

In 1976, having returned to Britain, he received a B.Phil. at St. Andrews' University for his thesis 'Montanism: Its Ancient Sources and Modern Interpretations'. He then went into parish work, serving successively as Curate of St. Mary's, Stoke Bishop, Bristol; Rector of Thrapston in Northamptonshire; and Rector of Barming in Kent. During this last incumbency he studied part-time at King's College, London, and in 2000 was awarded a Ph.D. for his thesis 'The Healing Ministry in the Pre-Nicene Church'. The substance of this thesis was later published as the book *Healing in the Early Church* by Paternoster (2009). Earlier he authored jointly with Roger Beckwith Latimer Studies 61, *The Water and the Wine: A Contribution to the Debate on Children and Holy Communion*, his special contribution being the chapters on the New Testament and Early Church. He has also written a number of articles.

Since 2003 he has been teaching at St. Andrew's Theological Seminary, Manila, the training college for clergy of the Episcopal Church in the Philippines and for some from the Iglesia Filipina Independiente. His courses have included Church History, pastoral subjects, missiology and, in 2014, Pauline Literature.

The seed thought for this present paper came from reading an article published in the Journal of Ecclesiastical History in 2006!

Introduction

We are very familiar with the New Testament and can easily verify its teachings, but what happened to these teachings subsequently? Were they upheld, diluted or discarded? In this paper we shall focus specifically on the apostle Paul's cardinal doctrine 'justification by faith'. The sixteenth-century Protestant Reformers thought it was ignored by the Church Fathers prior to Augustine (354-430). Within the last decade Daniel H. Williams in his article 'Justification by Faith: a Patristic Doctrine'[1] has said it was not noticed before Origen in the East (c.185-c.254) and Hilary of Poitiers (c.315-c.367) in the West. But with the doctrine's prominence in the Pauline letters, particularly Romans and Galatians, that would be surprising since there were earlier Fathers who deeply respected Paul and frequently quoted his statements as authoritative.

Joseph R. Dodson in his introduction to the symposium *Paul and the Second Century* cautions that while Paul had great influence on the second century, its writers rarely followed his theology but rather 'manipulated the meaning and appealed to the value of Paul to support their own arguments and to treat new ideas in new situations'.[2] Was this true of justification? In this paper we shall look first at the New Testament to see what Paul actually says before turning to the writings of six important early Fathers: Clement of Rome at the tail end of the first century, Ignatius of Antioch, Justin Martyr, Irenaeus and Clement of Alexandria from the second century, and Tertullian from the late second to the early third century.

---

[1] Daniel H. Williams, 'Justification by Faith: A Patristic Doctrine' in *Journal of Ecclesiastical History* 57.4, October 2006, pp 649-67.
[2] Michael F. Bird & Joseph R. Dodson eds, *Paul and the Second Century*, (London: T & T Clark, 2011), p 5.

The New Testament

Until recent decades there has been near consensus among Protestant scholars that, in contrast to the Rabbinic Judaism of his time which asserted one could only win God's approval by strict obedience to the tenets of the Torah, Paul declared that justification before God was only possible by faith in Christ crucified.[1]

As an example of this perspective let us take the detailed study of 'justification' by Leon Morris in *The Apostolic Preaching of the Cross*.[2] He points out that in both the Hebrew Old Testament and the Greek Septuagint (LXX) translation, one word (Heb. *tsedeq/tsedaqah*, Gk. *dikaiosunē*) is variously translated 'justification' and 'righteousness' in the English versions and its origin lay in the law courts. 'To justify' (*tsadaq, dikaioō*) meant 'to declare righteous', 'to acquit' (Exodus 23:7, Psalm 143:2), though other meanings developed later. To the Hebrew mind then God was fundamentally a God of law. His righteousness was shown in his acting consistently according to his moral law, unlike other gods whose actions were somewhat arbitrary, and he expected his people to conform to his laws or he must punish them. Turning to the apostle Paul, his strict adherence to the Jewish law as a zealous young Pharisee led him to reject Jesus as a false Messiah and to try to exterminate his followers. After his encounter with Christ on the Damascus road, however, he rejected this approach and articulated another. In Romans 1:16-17 he announces that the Christian Gospel offers salvation *to all who believe in Jesus Christ*, first Jews then also Gentiles. This Gospel he then unfolds in 3:21-28:

> But now, irrespective of law, the righteousness of God has been disclosed and is attested by the law and the prophets, the righteousness of God through faith in Jesus Christ for all who believe. For there is no distinction, since all have sinned and fall short of the glory of God; they are now justified by his grace as a gift, through the redemption that is in Christ Jesus, whom God put forward as a sacrifice of atonement by his blood, effective through faith. He did this to show his righteousness, because in his divine forbearance he had passed over the sins previously committed; it was to prove at the present time that he himself is righteous and that he justifies the one who has faith in Jesus. Then what becomes

---

[1] Galatians 2:16, 20; Romans 3:21-6.
[2] Leon Morris, *The Apostolic Preaching of the Cross* (London: Tyndale, 1955), chs. 7-8.

of boasting? It is excluded. By what law? By that of works? No, but by the law of faith. For we hold that a person is justified by faith apart from works prescribed by the law. (NRSV)

This passage has led to many debates but, for the present, it is sufficient to note the traditional Protestant interpretation that, because God's justice demanded punishment of sin while his mercy desired forgiveness, God put forward his Son to pay the penalty for human sin on our behalf. We lay hold of this salvation by faith. In Romans 4 Paul argues that, as God accounted Abraham righteous because of his faith (Genesis 15:6),[3] he accounts righteous all who have faith in Christ, who died and was raised to life again (cf. 1 Corinthians 15:3-4). What is this faith? Morris defines it as 'the enthusiastic allegiance to, and committal of, oneself to a person',[4] and says that the basic thought of the consequent righteousness is of 'a status conferred on men by God on the grounds of the atoning work of Christ'.[5]

In recent decades this traditional view has been challenged by a 'new perspective' based on an insight of Ed P. Sanders in his *Paul and Palestinian Judaism: a Comparison of Patterns of Religion*.[6] From exhaustive study of the literature of the Second Temple[7] Sanders concludes that the *Old* Covenant between God and Israel (Exodus 24:1-8) was recognized by the Jews of this period to be based on God's *grace*. Obedience to the law was not seen as earning God's acceptance as members of the Chosen Race but as the response to having been granted that membership. Sanders called this 'covenantal nomism'[8] but he did not, in the light of this, attempt a reinterpretation of Paul. James D. G. Dunn, however, took up the challenge. He suggested that what Paul was attacking as 'works of the law' was not obedience to the Torah in general but only to those tenets of the law emphasizing Israel's uniqueness, privileged status and separation from the Gentiles, such as circumcision and Sabbath observance.[9] But in fact Paul speaks of 'works of the law' without any hint of such a restricted purview. How emphatic, for instance, is his statement in Romans 3:20 that no-one will be justified in God's sight by works of the law since

---

[3]   Or imputed righteousness to Abraham.
[4]   Morris, *Apostolic Preaching*, p 243.
[5]   Morris, *Apostolic Preaching.*, p 258.
[6]   Ed P. Sanders, *Paul and Palestinian Judaism: a Comparison of Patterns of Religion* (London: SCM, 1977).
[7]   Jewish documents from 200 BC – AD 200.
[8]   From Gk. *nomos*, 'law'.
[9]   James D. G. Dunn, *The Theology of St Paul* (Edinburgh: T & T Clark, 1998), pp 355-6.

through the law comes knowledge of sin![10] Though the Old Covenant was based on God's grace it is surely possible that some of its adherents in Paul's day had lost sight of that and believed it was necessary to secure God's favour by strict observance of the law,[11] particularly in the light of such dire warnings as Deuteronomy 28:15-68.

This 'new perspective' has been further developed in the extensive writings of Bishop Tom Wright. He has presented his position most recently in *Justification: God's Plan and Paul's Vision*.[12] Discussing Romans 4 he sees Abraham's 'righteousness' as his right standing within his covenant with God (Genesis 15) and God's 'righteousness' as his 'unswerving commitment to be faithful to that covenant',[13] and he interprets 'Christ is the end of the law' (Romans 10:4) as meaning 'The Messiah is the culmination of the Torah, so that there may be *dikaiosunē*, covenant membership, for all who believe.'[14] Wright is not enthusiastic about 'imputed righteousness'; indeed he comments on Romans 6:3-4, 'It is not the 'righteousness' of Jesus Christ which is 'reckoned' to the believer. It is his death and resurrection.'[15] But such a statement scarcely invalidates the explicit claim in Romans 4:3 (quoting Genesis 15:6) that 'Abraham believed God, and it was reckoned to him as righteousness'. To many his most surprising point is that, since *pistis* can mean both 'faith' and 'faithfulness',[16] the Greek phrase *pisteōs Iēsou Christou* in Galatians 2:16 and Romans 3:22 should be rendered not as in our English versions 'faith in Jesus Christ' (in Gk. an 'objective genitive') but 'faithfulness of Jesus Christ' (a 'subjective genitive', cf. Romans 3:26, Galatians 2:20, 3:22, Philippians 3:9).[17] This faithfulness is shown by Christ's offering of himself on the cross, demonstrating such obedience to God as should have been offered by Israel. (He finds in the reference to Christ's obedience in Romans 5:19 confirmation of this interpretation,[18] though in fact the contrast there is between Christ and Adam not Christ and Israel.) The believer benefits from the fruits of Christ's faithfulness – his victory over sin and death – through faith and

---

[10] Cf. Romans 3:28, Galatians 2:16, 3:2, Philippians 3:9.
[11] Charles K. Barrett is clearly convinced this was the case – *Paul: An Introduction to His Thought* (London: Chapman, 1994), pp 77-80.
[12] Tom Wright, *Justification: God's Plan and Paul's Vision* (London: SPCK, 2009).
[13] Wright, *Justification*, pp 48-9.
[14] Wright, *Justification*, p 216.
[15] Wright, *Justification*, p 205.
[16] *Pistis* is translated 'faithfulness' in the LXX but 'faith' in the secular usage of Paul's time.
[17] Wright, *Justification*, pp 96-7, 178.
[18] Wright, *Justification*, p 83.

entering into his death and resurrection at baptism (Galatians 3:23-9, Romans 6:3-4).[19]

Wright's opting for the 'subjective genitive' in the specified verses is not in fact new. In 1967 George Howard argued forcefully for it in his article 'Notes and Observations on the 'Faith of Christ'',[20] and he mentions others before him. But a trenchant defence of the 'objective genitive' option was made by Arland J. Hultgren in his article 'The *Pistis Christou* Formulation in Paul' (1980).[21] He points out that, in the undisputed Pauline epistles (which include Romans, Galatians and Philippians), the Greek phrase *pistis Christou* and its equivalents always lacks the definite article before both nouns whereas, when Paul elsewhere intends a subjective genitive (e.g. in Romans 3:3 'the faith of God', and 4:12 'the faith of Abraham'), he almost invariably uses the article. Further, all the Pauline passages containing these phrases are focused on the justification of the believer on the basis of his faith and most contrast obtaining righteousness by works of the law with obtaining righteousness by faith. References to the faithfulness or even faith of Jesus would be out of place. These and his other arguments surely tell decisively against Paul's employing a subjective genitive in the passages under dispute.

[19] Wright, *Justification*, pp 202-3.
[20] George Howard, 'Notes and Observations on the "Faith of Christ"' in *Harvard Theological Review*, 60, pp 459-84.
[21] Arland J. Hultgren, 'The *Pistis Christou* Formulation in Paul' in *Novum Testamentum* XXII.3 (July 1980), pp 248-63.

Clement of Rome

The earliest post-biblical Christian writing is generally acknowledged to be a letter from the church in Rome to the church in Corinth, commonly known as 1 *Clement*, written it appears by the leading presbyter in Rome, Clement,[1] c.AD 96. Coming from the tail end of the first century it offers an interesting preliminary to our main study. Clement shows himself a great admirer of Paul for he tells of him just after speaking of the apostle Peter, calling him one of the 'noble figures of our own generation' and in glowing terms acclaiming his missionary zeal, endurance and martyrdom:

> Paul, because of jealousy and contention, has become the very type of endurance rewarded. He was in bonds seven times, he was exiled, he was stoned. He preached in the East and in the West, winning a noble reputation for his faith. He taught righteousness (*dikaiosunē*) to all the world; and after reaching the furthest limits of the West, and bearing his testimony before kings and rulers, he passed out of this world and was received into the holy place. In him we have one of the greatest of all examples of endurance. (5.5-7, tr. Staniforth)

Clement was clearly very familiar with Paul's 1 Corinthians. Later in his epistle he instructs the Corinthians to 'take up the epistle of the blessed apostle Paul' (47.1), and there are echoes of that epistle in chapters 24, 37 and 49 (in this last case he is surely quoting 1 Corinthians 13 from memory). We should expect Clement, living in Rome, also to be familiar with Paul's letter to the Romans, perhaps even with the original copy written some forty years before. That he was aware of its central doctrine is indicated by his declaration quoted above that Paul 'taught righteousness to the whole world' (5.7). In 1 *Clement* 10, like Paul in Romans 4, Clement focuses on Abraham and, though the two treatments are somewhat different, both quote Genesis 15:6.

Clement's purpose in writing his letter was to challenge and correct the vexed situation that had arisen in the Corinthian church, where some impetuous younger members had risen up and deposed duly elected presbyters who had long ministered faithfully (1, 44). In reproving the former Clement extols the qualities of faith and humility, pointing to Abraham as a paragon of faith (31.2) and to Jacob, fleeing from his brother Esau and serving his cousin Laban, as a model of humility (31.4). A line of celebrated descendants of the latter received

---

[1] Possibly to be identified with the Clement mentioned in Philippians 4:3.

glory, he says, 'not through themselves or their own works or the righteous actions which they did but through (God's) will' (32.4). And he drives home his point by declaring of his generation of Christians:

> And so we, having been called through his will in Christ Jesus are not justified (*dikaioumetha*) through ourselves or through our own wisdom or understanding or piety or works which we have done in holiness of heart but through faith, by which the almighty God has justified (*edikaiōsen*) all who have existed from the beginning,[2] to whom be the glory for ever and ever. Amen. (32.4, tr. Holmes)

Ernst Dassmann comments, 'This is unambiguous Pauline *sola fideism* without any reduction'.[3] But Clement is clearly anxious not to appear to be disparaging good works for he immediately continues:

> What then shall we do, brothers? Shall we idly abstain from doing good and forsake love? May the Master never allow this to happen, at least to us; but let us hasten with earnestness and zeal to accomplish every good work. (33.1, Holmes, cf. 34.4)

Clement sees it is vital that faith should issue in good deeds as emphasised by James,[4] an epistle he may have known,[5] and indeed emphasised by Paul himself.[6] A little before the passages we have quoted Clement says that Christians should be 'justified by works' (30.3), but there his contrast is not between works and faith, but works and empty words. Later again he focuses on the importance of good behaviour as a prerequisite for enjoying the blessings of Christ's return:

> Let us strive, therefore, to be found in the number of those who wait for him, that we may share in the promised gifts. But how shall this be, beloved? If our mind be fixed by means of faith on God; if we seek what is pleasing and acceptable to him; if we perform what is proper to his faultless will and follow the path of truth, casting from

---

[2]   *Ap aionos* more accurately translated 'down the ages' (Joseph B. Lightfoot).

[3]   Ernst Dassmann, *Der Stachel im Fleisch: Paulus in der frühchristlichen Literatur bis Irenaüs* (Münster: Aschendorff, 1979), p 85. Consonant with Clement's view here is his earlier statement, when relating the story of Rahab's scarlet thread in Jericho (Joshua 2): 'Thus they made it manifest that redemption should flow through the blood of the Lord to all them that believe and hope in God' (12.7) which Andreas Lindemann thinks may be 'a typical expression of Clement's own theological position' – *Paulus, Apostel und Lehrer der Kirche* (Tübingen: Mohr, 1999), p 266.

[4]   James 2:18-26.

[5]   It was almost certainly known to Hermas in Rome in the first half of the second century – see S. Laws, *Commentary on the Epistle of James* (London: A & C Black, 1980), pp 20-23.

[6]   Ephesians 2:8-10.

us all injustice and wickedness... (35.4-5, tr. Glimm, Fathers of the Church)

Here again he is saying that right action will stem from faith in God and seeking his will. So Leslie W. Barnard is surely wrong when he says that Clement (like Ignatius of Antioch) has 'no real appreciation of the Pauline 'righteousness by faith''.[7] Dassmann makes a fairer assessment when he says that the Roman congregation in whose name Clement wrote took up Paul's theology but, connected also to numerous threads from other traditions, blended it into a 'post-apostolic, early catholic theology'.[8]

---

[7]   Leslie W. Barnard, *Studies in the Apostolic Fathers and their Background* (New York: Schoken, 1966), p 28.

[8]   Dassman, *Stachel*, p 94.

Ignatius of Antioch

According to Eusebius, Ignatius was the third bishop of Antioch (Peter being the first).[1] He is known from seven letters attributed to him,[2] written c.AD 110 in an exuberant style now recognized to be 'Asianic' rhetoric.

It has been surmised that there had been severe conflict in the church in Antioch between Judaeo-Christians, who prized the Gospel of Matthew, and Hellenists who adhered to a form of Pauline Christianity, and that Ignatius had been denounced by the former to the Roman authorities, who then sent him for execution in Rome.[3] Careful study of what Ignatius says about his church suggests however that it had been the victim of general persecution.[4] Nevertheless, while he may not have been in open conflict with Judaeo-Christians, he shows himself resolutely opposed to any attempt to lead the church back to Judaism.[5] He deeply admired the apostle Paul whom he sought to imitate,[6] and clearly he knew 1 Corinthians, Ephesians, Philippians and perhaps other Paulines.[7]

Often Ignatius mentions together faith and love as the key Christian qualities.[8] In his *Ephesians* 14.1-2, for instance, after mentioning other aspects of the Christian life, he writes:

None of these things escapes you if you have perfect faith and love

---

[1] Eusebius, *Historia Ecclesiastica* 3.22, 36.

[2] Considering in this article just the middle recension of these which has long been generally accepted as genuine.

[3] Simon Tugwell, *The Apostolic Fathers* (London: Continuum, 1989), p 123, Christine Trevett, *A study of Ignatius of Antioch in Syria and Asia* (Lewiston: Mullen, 1992), pp 180-3.

[4] *Romans* 9 tells of the church as having Christ as head because Ignatius has been removed from leadership, *Romans* 10 refers to others sent ahead of Ignatius to Rome 'for the glory of God' – martyrdom? *Philadelphians* 11 speaks of Rheus Agathopou, 'one of the elect, who has followed after me from Syria, and abjured this earthly life' – clearly another martyr. *Smyrnaeans* 11 speaks of 'the restoration of peace ...their recovery of their proper numbers, and ...their re-establishment as a corporate body again' (tr. Staniforth; cf. *Philadelphians* 10, *Polycarp* 7).

[5] *Magnesians* 8, 10, *Philadelphians* 6, 8-9.

[6] 'You are fellow-initiates of Paul, who was sanctified, who also was approved [or 'martyred'– *memarturēmenou*], who is deservedly blessed – may I be found in his footsteps when I reach God!' (*Ephesians* 12.2, tr. Holmes)

[7] *Ephesians* 18.1 echoes 1 Corinthians 1:18-20; the instruction in *Polycarp* 5 to tell Christian men 'to love their wives as the Lord loves the Church' recalls Paul's extended simile in Ephesians 5:25-33; the present article suggests Ignatius had taken to heart Philippians 3:10-12; and the reference to justification in *Philadelphians* 8.2 could well indicate knowledge of Romans or Galatians.

[8] *Ephesians* 1.1, 9.1, 14.1-2, *Magnesians* 1.2, 13, *Trallians* 8.1 *et passim*.

in Jesus Christ, which are the beginning and end of life: the beginning is faith, the end is love; these two, existing in unity, are God; all other things leading to nobility follow from them.[9]

Sometimes he speaks of faith separately. He knows of course that Jesus Christ suffered for our sins (*Smyrnaeans* 7.1), and speaks to the Trallians of 'Jesus Christ who died for us, that by believing in his death you may escape dying' (*Trallians* 2.1, cf. *Smyrnaeans* 1.1, 2). Elsewhere he declares, 'Let no one be deceived: even heavenly powers and the glory of angels[10] and the rulers, both visible and invisible, if they do not believe in the blood of Christ, are also subject to judgment' (*Smyrnaeans* 6.1). But only in one passage does he make an explicit connection between faith and justification. He has been telling the church at Philadelphia to shun Judaism and then quotes, it seems, the very words of some Judaeo-Christians:

I heard some say, "If I do not find (it) in the archives,[11] I do not believe it in the gospel"... But for me, the archives are Jesus Christ, the inviolable archives are his cross and death and his resurrection and faith through him, in which, through your prayers, I want to be justified (*dikaiōthēnai*). (*Philadelphians* 8.2)

Andreas Lindemann sees here a reference to Paul's key doctrine.[12] But if then Ignatius would sympathise with Paul's statement in Philippians 3:8-9 that his righteousness before God came not from observance of the law but by faith in Christ, time and again his sentiments echo rather Paul's desire in Philippians 3:10-12 to share in the sufferings and death of Christ that somehow he may attain the resurrection from the dead. Ignatius passionately desires martyrdom at Rome, seeing it as his assured way of attaining Christian discipleship and securing salvation.[13] Nowhere is this stated more emphatically than in his letter to the Romans where he pleads with them not to try to avert his death in the arena:

---

[9] Tr. William R. Schoedel, *Ignatius of Antioch* (Philadelphia: Fortress, 1985). All quotations of Ignatius' epistles in the text will be taken from this translation unless otherwise indicated.

[10] Schoedel translates the Greek literally here but perhaps this phrase would be better rendered 'and the glorious angels'.

[11] *Archeiois*, a Hellenistic Jewish conception of the Old Testament. See Schoedel, *Ignatius*, 17, pp 207-9.

[12] Lindemann, *Paulus*, p 271. Dassmann observes from this passage that Ignatius' charismatic preaching was not based on the New Testament documents but looked straight back to Christ's life on earth; Christ, his death and resurrection, and faith in him were his documents (Dassmann, *Stachel*, pp 134-5).

[13] *Trallians* 12.2, *Romans* 4.1-3, 5.2-3, 6-7, *Smyrnaeans* 4.2, *Polycarp* 7.1.

Let me be food of wild beasts through whom it is possible to attain God; I am the wheat of God, and I am ground by the teeth of wild beasts that I may be found pure bread; instead entice the wild beasts that they may become my tomb and leave behind no part of my body that when I fall asleep, I may burden no one. Then I shall truly be a disciple of Jesus Christ when the world will not even see my body. Pray Christ for me that by these means I may be found a sacrifice of God. (4.1-2)

May I benefit from the wild beasts prepared for me, and I pray that they will be found prompt with me, whom I shall even entice to devour me promptly ... now I begin to be a disciple. May nothing of things visible or invisible envy me, that I may attain Jesus Christ. Fire and cross, and packs of wild beasts, the wrenching of bones, the mangling of limbs, the grinding of my whole body, evil punishments of the devil – let these come upon me, only that I may attain Jesus Christ! (5.2-3)

Why does he, a bishop from Antioch in Syria, to whom churches along his route send respectful delegations, have the extraordinary idea that he must fight with beasts and die in the arena in Rome to attain true Christian discipleship?

A notable feature of almost all Ignatius' letters is his self-denigration as the 'last' or 'least' of all the members of the Syrian church, unworthy to be called a member.[14] Here he clearly echoes Paul's self-deprecation, even to the extent of referring to his new birth as being like an abortion.[15] It seems natural then to conclude that Ignatius, like Paul himself, had, before becoming a Christian, been an opponent of the church,[16] or was guilty of some other major misdemeanour. On account of this, when he had been elevated to leadership of the church in Antioch, some of his opponents may well have flung at him the assertion that he was 'not worthy to be called a disciple of Christ'. He then seized on this chance of martyrdom as a means of indisputably establishing his Christian discipleship. So Trevett is surely right to conclude that, in practice, Ignatius had little conception of salvation by God's grace.[17]

---

[14] *Romans 9.2, Ephesians 21.2, Trallians 13.1, Smyrnaeans 11.1, Magnesians* 14.
[15] Ignatius, *Romans* 9.2, cf. 1 Corinthians 15:8.
[16] *Pace* Schoedel, *Ignatius*, 13.
[17] Trevett, *Study*, p 19. Dassmann, following Bultmann, recognises that the language of Pauline soteriology, of sin and justification, scarcely features at all in Ignatius' theology (Dassmann, *Stachel*, pp 140-141).

Justin Martyr

While the Apostolic Fathers were concerned with internal matters of the Church, the Apologists, who succeeded them, were occupied with presenting a reasoned defence of Christianity to the wider world. The greatest of them in the second century was Justin (c.AD 100-165). Born a pagan in Flavia Neapolis (modern Nablus) in Samaria, he received a Hellenistic education and came to delight in philosophy, sampling in turn Stoic, Aristotelian and Pythagorean teachers before settling on Platonism.[1] He was converted after a discussion with an elderly Christian man who directed him to study the Old Testament prophecies (presumably about the Messiah).[2] Justin then proclaimed Christianity as the true philosophy, the completion of what Plato and the other philosophers had taught.[3]

In the Greco-Roman world of that time *logos* meant both inward thought (reason) and its outward expression (word). Middle Platonism, which Justin had imbibed, taught that the *Logos* was God's personal reason in which all people partake; he now proclaimed that in Jesus Christ it had taken human form.[4] He writes:

> His word of truth and wisdom is more blazing and bright than the might of the sun, and it penetrates the very depths of the heart and mind. (*Dialogue* 121.2)[5]

Perhaps then it is not surprising to hear Justin referring to regeneration, through baptism in the three-fold Name, as 'illumination' of the mind.[6] In his works he freely quotes from the Synoptic Gospels and occasionally also the Fourth Gospel from which he surely learnt to identify Jesus with the *Logos*.

But Justin never mentions Paul. Hans von Campenhausen suggests this might be due to Paul's having been adopted as 'the Apostle' by the heretics Marcion and Valentinus,[7] both of whom were contemporaries

---

[1]   Justin, *Dialogue with Trypho* 2.
[2]   *Dialogue* 7-8.
[3]   *2 Apology* 13.
[4]   *1 Apology* 5.
[5]   This and subsequent quotations from *Dialogue* are taken from the translation in Fathers of the Church. Is Justin's wording here influenced by Hebrews 4:12?
[6]   *1 Apology* 61.
[7]   Hans von Campenhausen, *The Formation of the Christian Bible*, tr. John A. Baker (London: A & C Black, 1972), pp 177-8. See also Nicholas Perrin, 'Paul and Valentinian Interpretation' in Bird & Dodson, *Paul*, ch. 7 for more details of Valentinus' use of Paul.

of Justin in Rome. Marcion indeed, regarding Paul as the only apostle who had recognised the radical dichotomy between the Jewish law and the Gospel, took ten Pauline epistles, considerably edited, alongside an abridged version of Luke, as his canon of Scripture. Justin actually wrote against Marcion (Eusebius, *Historia Ecclesiastica* 4.11.8) but this work has not survived. Campenhausen points out, however, that the fact that Marcion had mutilated the Paulines meant their unmutilated form might still be regarded as trustworthy and acceptable.[8] Anyway, why should Justin refer to Paul by name? There was no occasion for doing so in his *Apologies*, and in his *Dialogue with Trypho*, where there seem to be a number of echoes of Paul: to name one whom the Jews regarded as an 'apostate rabbi' would only have discredited his case.

Justin is in no doubt that, since the coming of Jesus, the Old Covenant is obsolete. He argues this in *Dialogue* 11, quoting Jeremiah's prophecy of a New Covenant (Jeremiah 31:31-2), and concludes:

> We (Christians) have been led to God through this crucified Christ, and we are the true spiritual Israel, and the descendants of Juda, Jacob, Isaac, and Abraham, who, though uncircumcised, was approved and blessed by God because of his faith and was called the father of many nations. All this shall be proved as we proceed with our discussion.

This is Justin's first reference to Abraham, and the points he makes about him appear to echo Paul's statements in Romans 4:3, 11, 17. He speaks further of Abraham in *Dialogue* 23:

> When Abraham himself was still uncircumcised, he was justified and blessed by God because of his faith in him, as the Scriptures tell us. Furthermore, the Scriptures and the facts of the case force us to admit that Abraham received circumcision for a sign, not for justification itself.

Here he follows quite closely Paul's argument in Romans 4:9-11 (using *dikaioō* and *dikaiosunē*). He goes on to make his own point that, had circumcision had merit in itself, this would discriminate against women for they could not receive such circumcision. In *Dialogue* 92, quoting again Genesis 15:6, he reiterates that Abraham was considered righteous not because of his circumcision but because of his faith, and says that Christians, though uncircumcised, have by their faith in God through Christ, a circumcision of the heart – a thought derived perhaps

---

8   Campenhausen, *Formation*, p 180.

from Romans 2:9.[9] One more emphatic restatement of justification by faith is found in *Dialogue* 119. Justin has pointed out that other worthies of old had fathered individual nations but Abraham was to be father of many nations, and he continues:

> What greater favour, then, did Christ bestow on Abraham? This: that he likewise called with his voice, and commanded him to leave the land wherein he dwelt. And with that same voice he has also called all of us, and we have abandoned our former way of life in which we used to practice evils common to the rest of the world. And we shall inherit the Holy Land together with Abraham, receiving our inheritance for all eternity, because by our similar faith we have become children of Abraham. For, just as he believed the voice of God, and was justified thereby, so have we believed the voice of God (which was spoken again to us by the Prophets and the Apostles of Christ), and have renounced even to death all worldly things.

This passage surely echoes the thoughts of Galatians 3:6-9. Paul Foster, however, noting the differences in detail between the two passages, believes they are independent meditations by Justin and Paul on Genesis 15:6.[10] But this scarcely gives credit to the originality of Paul's thought in deriving his doctrine of justification by faith from the case of Abraham.[11]

As with Paul, Justin believed it was faith in Christ's sacrifice on the cross that brought salvation. This he states repeatedly in many different ways. He declares penitents are 'no longer made pure by the blood of goats and sheep or by the ashes of a heifer, or by the offerings of fine flour, but by faith through the blood and the death of Christ who suffered death for this precise purpose' (*Dialogue* 13).[12] Again, 'Now, just as the blood of the Passover saved those who were in Egypt, so also shall the blood of Christ rescue from death all those who have believed in him' (*Dialogue* 111). He finds the shape of the cross prefigured in Moses'

---

[9] Though Paul Foster correctly points out that this phrase was well-known in the Old Testament (Deuteronomy 10:16 *et passim*), 'Justin and Paul' in Bird & Dodson, *Paul*, p 118.

[10] In Bird & Dodson, *Paul*, pp 122-3.

[11] Paul maintained that the Gospel he taught came by direct revelation from Christ (Galatians 1:12). Foster is unconvinced that Justin drew on Paul's writings at all, but many scholars disagree. Dassmann, for instance, points out that when in *Dialogue* 27.3 Justin uses the same Psalm and Isaiah quotations as in Romans 3:12-17], and when in *Dialogue* 39.1-2 he expresses the lament of Elijah against Israel and God's answer in a way in which several details differ from the LXX but agree with Romans 11:2-5, one cannot doubt that Justin knew Romans (Dassmann, *Stachel*, p 245).

[12] Cf. Hebrews 9:11-14.

hands held up by Hur and Aaron until Israel prevailed over Amalek (Exodus 17:9-12 – *Dialogue* 90), and in the red cord Joshua's spies gave the harlot Rahab (Joshua 2:18), 'a symbol of the blood of Christ, by which those of every nationality who were once fornicators and sinful are redeemed, receiving pardon of their past sin and avoiding all sin in the future' (*Dialogue* 111). He quotes at length Isaiah 53 as a prophecy of Christ's sacrifice (*1 Apology* 50-1, *Dialogue* 13), and he expounds Psalm 22, pointing to gospel material to show its fulfilment (*Dialogue* 98-106).

Now he also said that, for believers, the blood of Christ avails for the forgiveness of past sins but obedience must follow, leading to eternal salvation (*1 Apology* 8, 10, 14, 61, 65, *Dialogue* 44, 111). From such passages and from the fact that, of the documents of the New Testament, Justin actually quotes only from the gospels,[13] George T. Purves concluded that for Justin, 'Faith is belief in the truth of Christ's word rather than the acceptance of a finished redemption'.[14] But, in the light of Justin's huge emphasis on the value of Christ's sacrificial death, this is surely not so. Certainly in his *Apologies* Justin always wishes to paint Christians as exemplary citizens committed to good works. But then in the New Testament, that Christians will be judged on their good deeds is not only stated in more traditional Jewish Christian documents (Matthew 25:31-46, Revelation 20:12) but also by Paul himself in 2 Corinthians 5:10. How can this be reconciled with justification by faith? One might say that true faith is always shown by works (James 2:26), or perhaps surmise that Christ's death avails for believers' entry into heaven, whilst their performance as Christians determines the place they occupy there.[15] It seems Justin had not teased this out.

One or two matters remain to be considered. Justin was trained as a philosopher before he became a Christian and had learnt to view reason as of eminent value. He believed, it seems, that those who lived by reason would always choose good.[16] Others, led by unreasonable passion engendered by wicked demons posing as gods, engaged in such activities as the persecution of Christians.[17] Those living by reason before the incarnation, even if considered atheists in their time, were

---

[13] Especially in *1 Apology* 15-17.
[14] George T. Purves, *The Testimony of Justin Martyr to Early Christianity* (London: Nisbet, 1888), Lecture IV.
[15] A suggestion put to me by Dr. Leon Morris when Principal of Ridley College, Melbourne.
[16] *1 Apology* 2, 12.
[17] *1 Apology* 5.

'Christians before Christ'.[18] Paul too realized there were good people in the world outside the realm of God's people that God might judge positively (Romans 2:14-16). The justice of God had to be upheld.

Since Adam's first sin, Justin declared, humans have been 'subject to death and the deceit of the serpent, each man having sinned by his own fault' (*Dialogue* 88). Here he echoes Paul's statement that, 'Just as sin came into the world through one man, and death came through sin, and so death spread to all because all have sinned' (Romans 5:12). Where they part company is in their estimate of how far humans retained the ability to do right. Paul speaks of humans as 'slaves to sin' (6:17, 20, 7:14) and sees himself as unable to do the good things he wishes (7:15-20). Justin believes humans remain free and can choose good (1 *Apology* 43, *Dialogue* 88), though they have to contend against the influence of evil demons (1 *Apology* 5). Paul and Justin also differ in their estimate of the Jewish law. Paul sees it had a valid role as a disciplinary tutor until Christ came (Galatians 3:24) and, though through it sin sprang to life, in itself it is essentially 'holy, just and good' and 'spiritual' (Romans 7:7-14). Justin, however, while recognizing some of its precepts are 'good, pious and just' (*Dialogue* 45), speaks generally in negative terms. 'Not because he needed such sacrifices,' he says to the Jew Trypho, 'did God command you to sacrifice to him, but because of the sins of your people, especially their sins of idolatry' (*Dialogue* 22). And again, 'Because of the hardness of your hearts God imposed such commandments upon you through Moses in order that, by observing these many precepts, you might have him constantly before your eyes and refrain from every unjust or impious act' (*Dialogue* 46).[19]

Justin, however, concurs with Paul's argument in Galatians 3:10-14 that Christ by being cursed through being crucified ('hanged on a tree', Deuteronomy 21:23), took upon himself the curse that lay on the whole Jewish race through its failure perfectly to observe the Law (Deuteronomy 27:26); indeed Justin believed this curse extended to the whole Gentile world as well; and he saw Deuteronomy 21:23 as also a prediction of the curse being pronounced on Christians in Jewish synagogues in his time (*Dialogue* 94-96).

Thus, in a number of related matters Justin, a century later than Paul, would seem to be using the apostle's arguments to show the inadequacy of Judaism, adapting them to the situation of his time. One cannot fairly accuse him of preaching 'another gospel'.

---

[18] 1 *Apology* 46.
[19] Cf. *Dialogue* 18, 19, 20, 43, *et passim*.

Irenaeus

Irenaeus is generally considered the greatest Christian theologian of the second century. Born perhaps c.AD 130 he appears to have been brought up in Asia Minor, where as a young man he listened eagerly to the elderly Polycarp.[1] In the 180s, as bishop of Lyons, he wrote his great five-volume work *Refutation and Overthrow of Falsely Named Knowledge* which has come down to us in a literal Latin translation under the title *Against the Heresies*. It is an important source of information about various Gnostic sects and Marcion, but it also gives us much information about the Church of his time and embodies his own somewhat distinctive theological stance. His later work *Demonstration of the Apostolic Teaching*, addressed to a certain Marcianus, is much shorter and has come down to us in an Armenian translation.

If Justin's quotations from our New Testament are restricted very largely to the Synoptic Gospels, Irenaeus ranges far wider. If rehabilitation were needed for Paul because he had been patronized by Marcion and some Gnostics, Irenaeus effectively provides this. Though he will not allow Marcion's claim that Paul alone among the apostles knew the truth, and points out that Paul himself acknowledged the other apostles,[2] he stresses Paul's close connection with Luke[3] and refutes those who deny Paul's apostleship.[4] He also constantly quotes Paul, basing many of his own statements on those of the apostle.[5]

Irenaeus' cardinal doctrine of 'recapitulation' (Lat. *recapitulatio*, Gk. *anakephalaiōsis*) has been described as 'an attempt by Irenaeus to embody the whole of the Biblical proclamation about the work of Christ in a single word'.[6] This term he appears to take from Paul's use of the

---

[1]   *Against Heresies* 3.3.4.
[2]   *Against Heresies* 3.13.1-2.
[3]   *Against Heresies* 3.14.
[4]   *Against Heresies* 3.15.1.
[5]   Cf. Campenhausen's verdict: 'Irenaeus in no way shares the prevailing tendency to rank Paul below the first apostles or even to ignore him altogether. On the contrary, it is on Paul in particular that he bases his position, feeling himself to be the legitimate heir of Pauline theology', (Campenhausen, *Formation*, p 193). Blackwell acknowledges that for Irenaeus Paul's letters are 'a primary authoritative source since he is 'the Apostle'' and that they played an important role in the exposition of his own theology (Ben C. Blackwell, 'Paul and Irenaeus' in Bird & Dodson, *Paul*, pp 193, 206).
[6]   Gustaf Wingren, *Man and the incarnation: A study in the biblical theology of Irenaeus*, Eng. tr. (Edinburgh: Oliver & Boyd, 1959), p 80.

cognate verb *anakephalaioō* in Ephesians 1:10.[7] It has, in fact, a breadth of meanings. Denis Minns tells us its origin lies in rhetoric where it means 'to sum up an argument by going back over the principal points'.[8] Eric Osborn finds in Irenaeus' use of recapitulation no less than eleven ideas.[9] Irenaeus does indeed use this term very frequently but his primary assertion by it is to say that Christ 'went through all the experiences of Adam but with the opposite result'.[10] Let us look at some of his actual statements:

> For as by one man's disobedience sin entered, and death obtained [a place] through sin; so also by the obedience of one man, righteousness having been introduced shall cause life to fructify in those persons who in times past were dead.[11] And as the protoplast himself, Adam, had his substance from untilled and as yet virgin soil...so did He who is the Word, recapitulating Adam in Himself, rightly receive a birth, enabling Him to gather up Adam [into Himself], from Mary, who was as yet a virgin. (*Against Heresies* 3.21.10)[12]

> For by summing up in Himself the whole human race from the beginning to the end, He has also summed up its death. From this it is clear that the Lord suffered death, in obedience to his Father, upon that day on which Adam died while he disobeyed God. Now he died on the same day in which he did eat. For God said, "In that day on which ye shall eat of it, ye shall die by death." The Lord, therefore recapitulating in Himself this day, underwent His sufferings upon the day preceding the Sabbath, that is, the sixth day of the creation, on which day man was created; thus granting him a second creation by means of His passion, which is that [creation] out of death. (*Against Heresies* 5.23.2)

Irenaeus speaks similarly of the obedient Mary recapitulating the disobedient Eve,[13] Christians recapitulating (repeating) the faith of

---

[7] Jesus' manifestation from heaven was '"to gather all things in one," and to raise up anew all flesh of the whole human race...'*Against Heresies* 1.10.1 (Ante-Nicene Fathers), cf. v.20.2.

[8] Denis Minns, *Irenaeus* (London: Chapman, 1994), p 92.

[9] Eric Osborn, *Irenaeus of Lyons* (Cambridge: University Press, 2001), pp 97-8.

[10] John Lawson, *The Biblical Theology of Saint Irenaeus* (London: Epworth, 1948), p 143.

[11] Romans 5:19.

[12] This and subsequent quotations from *Against Heresies* are taken from the *Ante-Nicene Fathers* I 1885 (1995).

[13] *Against Heresies* 3.22.4, 5.19.1, *Demonstration* 33.

Abraham,[14] and a beast in Revelation recapitulating (summing up) all sorts of evil.[15]

But Irenaeus is not so enamoured with this concept that he completely loses sight of Paul's doctrine of justification; indeed he sees justification as a fruit of recapitulation:

> For as by the disobedience of the one man who was originally moulded from virgin soil, the many were made sinners, and forfeited life; so was it necessary that, by the obedience of one man, who was originally born from a virgin, many should be justified (*dikaiōthēnai*) and receive salvation...God recapitulated in himself the ancient formation of man, that he might kill sin, deprive death of its power, and vivify man; and therefore his works are true. (*Against Heresies* 3.18.7)[16]

That this justification is mediated through faith is amply testified in other statements by Irenaeus. He quotes Romans 3:30 saying that God will justify both the Jews and Gentiles through faith (*Against Heresies* 3.10.2, 5.22.1). In 3.16.9 he quotes Romans 5:6-10, including the phrase 'justified by his blood', and concludes from this and other statements of Paul that 'Jesus Christ, the Son of God... did by suffering reconcile us to God, and rose from the dead.'[17] Clearly he recognizes salvation results from repentance and faith in the Lamb of God who takes away the sin of the world (*Against Heresies* 3.10.2). Elsewhere he holds up Abraham as the great exemplar of faith, to whom faith was counted by God as righteousness (quoting Romans 4:3), and concludes 'for faith towards God justifies a man' (*Against Heresies* 4.5.3-5, cf. 4.16.2, 5.32.2, *Demonstration* 24, 35). Irenaeus recognizes that some will perish for lack of faith (*Against Heresies* 4.28.3), but he will not accept that it is God who hardens people's hearts, rather God knows their unbelief and then turns his face from them (4.29.1-2).

But this is not the whole picture. Irenaeus believes all human beings are aware of a basic morality through natural law. This he considers to be tantamount to the Decalogue. Those who fail to obey it,

---

[14] *Demonstration* 95.
[15] *Against Heresies* 5.29.2 – Revelation 13:11-18.
[16] Rolf Noormann notes that, through the combination here of Romans 5:19 and Romans 8:3, Irenaeus' common Adam-Christ theme is implicit – *Irenäus als Paulusinterpret* (Tübingen: Mohr, 1994), p 146 – but he ignores here the terminology of justification surely taken from Romans 5:9, cf. *Against Heresies* 3.16.9 where the phrase 'justified by his blood' is actually quoted.
[17] He is protesting against Gnostic claims such as that the heavenly Christ descended on the human Jesus.

he says, cannot be saved (*Against Heresies* 4.15.1). Those who, in the time before the laws of the Old Covenant were given, kept it he speaks of as being 'justified' by so doing (4.13.1). But this surely is not far from Paul's view in Romans 2:14-15.

The Marcionites rejected both the Old Covenant and the inferior god whom they said enacted it. In response Irenaeus stresses it is one and the same God who was behind both the Old and New Covenants. Christ's teaching did not overturn the precepts of the past but extended and developed them. So Christ was 'fulfilling the law, and implanting in us the varied righteousness of the law' (4.13.1). This does not mean that Christians are slaves by taking on the yoke of the law (like the Jews, cf. Galatians 4:24-5) but in our freedom through Christ we follow higher standards 'so that no one who is converted shall appear unworthy to him who set him free' (4.13.2). From Paul's likening himself to an athlete rigorously training his body lest in the end he might be disqualified (1 Corinthians 9:27) he concludes, 'This able wrestler, therefore exhorts us to struggle for immortality, that we may be crowned, and may deem the crown precious, namely, that which is acquired by our struggle, but which does not encircle us of its own accord'. This means we should strive to love God more (4.37.7). Any note of uncertainty about salvation here surely derives from the apostle's own statement. In *Demonstration* 41 Irenaeus reiterates the need for Christian effort leading to salvation when he says it is for those who have believed and persisted in the faith in holiness, righteousness and patient endurance that God has promised 'eternal life by the resurrection of the dead'.[18] This statement is no doubt influenced by Christ's own teaching that 'he who endures to the end will be saved' (Matthew 24:13). It is not really a contradiction of justification by faith but it insists one must continue in faith, showing forth its fruits of holiness and righteousness, right to the end.

Irenaeus viewed the Old Testament laws variously. There were the essential precepts of the Decalogue (*Against Heresies* 4.15.1). Other statutes such as circumcision and Sabbath observance were signs, circumcision for instance being the physical sign of being a descendant of Abraham (4.16.1). Other laws ('laws of bondage') were added gradually for the instruction and punishment of Israel (4.16.5); God did not really need their animal sacrifices but their obedience (4.17.1). Who

---

[18] Joseph Armitage Robinson's English translation of *Demonstration* has been made easily accessible by being printed in the front of Iain M. MacKenzie's *Irenaeus's Demonstration of the Apostolic Preaching: a theological commentary and translation* (Aldershot: Ashgate, 2002).

then before Christ's coming could be saved? All who from the beginning 'have both feared and loved God, and practiced justice and piety towards their neighbours, and have earnestly desired to see Christ, and to hear His voice. Wherefore He shall, at His second coming, first rouse from their sleep all persons of this description, and shall raise them up, as well as the rest who shall be judged, and give them a place in His kingdom' (4.22.2). This is how he envisages a just God will act.

It is sometimes complained that Irenaeus loses sight of faith as trust in God, replacing it by adhering to the 'rule of faith' – a statement of belief in God the Father, Jesus his Son, and the Holy Spirit which amounts to an informal equivalent to the Apostles' Creed. By Irenaeus' time a threefold confession of faith such as this was made at baptism. It distinguished orthodox Christianity from the beliefs of the heretics (*Demonstration* 3). Whilst it became a formalized statement of faith it did not exclude personal trust in the triune God at the same time.

As we have seen above, the 'new perspective' on Pauline theology focuses on faithfulness of Christ in offering himself as a sacrifice for sin on Calvary. Tom Wright sees this as the supreme demonstration of Christ's obedience to God's will in contrast to Israel's disobedience. Irenaeus likewise majors on Christ's supreme act of obedience in dying on the cross, but he contrasts it rather with the disobedience of Adam (like Paul in Romans 5:12-19, cf. 1 Corinthians 15:45-9). His concept of recapitulation would seem to be a legitimate elaboration, rather than a distortion of Pauline theology. If the cross and death of Christ do not stand at the centre of Irenaeus' soteriology this may be due, as Dassmann suggests, to the influence of the Fourth Gospel which, coming from Asia Minor, influenced the theology of the church there, emphasing the incarnation of the Logos (John 1:14).[19]

---

[19] Dassmann, *Stachel*, p 310.

Clement of Alexandria

While Irenaeus was a bishop of the Church, Clement was an independent academic teacher, widely read in the Greek philosophers and poets and many other writers. Like Justin, in searching for the truth, he had resorted to a succession of teachers before finding in Alexandria one who really satisfied him – Pantaenus, a learned Christian teacher, a Hebrew from Palestine who was once a Stoic. Eusebius says Clement succeeded Pantaenus as head of the catechetical school in Alexandria in the 190s.[1] In his *Exhortation* his aim was to convert to Christianity those who had received a Hellenic education, in his *Instructor* he endeavoured to give new converts elementary instruction in the faith and virtuous living, and in his longer unsystematic *Miscellanies* he sought to lead thoughtful believers into full Christian maturity. We also have his sermon *Who is the Rich Man that is Saved?* and other works. Clement draws on a vast array of sources; he quotes from the Pauline literature almost as often as the gospels, calling Paul 'the Apostle' and clearly regarding his words as authoritative.[2]

In the first half of the second century a number of influential Gnostics taught in Alexandria, particularly Basilides and Valentinus. Their amalgams of Christianity, Greek philosophy and other elements appear to have attracted a considerable following. Clement repeatedly criticized their teachings, regarding them as building on the foundation of Christ structures of 'stubble, wood and hay'.[3] Yet he maintained that philosophy should be prized not rejected by Christians, seeing it as an instructor preparing the Greeks for Christ as the Torah had prepared the Jews (Galatians 3:24).[4]

Clement devotes considerable attention to the matter of faith. He says that God has given humans free will, and so faith is a matter of rational choice in response to hearing the Gospel (*Miscellanies* 2.2, 4, 6 referring to Romans 10:17); it leads to salvation. *Instructor* 1.6 is largely

---

[1]   Eusebius, *Historia Ecclesiastica* 6.6, though some scholars today, perhaps because of Clement's independence of thought, believe he may have opened his own school – see Walter H. Wagner, 'Clement of Alexandria' in *Encyclopedia of early Christianity*, ed. Everett Ferguson, 2nd edn (New York: Garland, 1999).

[2]   See for example *Instructor* 1.6 with its quotations particularly from Galatians and 1 Corinthians but also other epistles.

[3]   *Miscellanies* 5.4 referring to Paul's statement in 1 Corinthians 3:11-12.

[4]   *Miscellanies* 1.5. He even speaks of philosophy 'justifying' the Greeks, meaning it prepared them for Christ (1.4-5, 20).

devoted to the matter of faith. Rejecting the Gnostic claim that in 1 Corinthians 3:2 'milk' refers to the 'common faith' of ordinary Christians while 'meat' to their special knowledge, Clement declares milk is 'perfect nourishment' for new-born babies, 'the knowledge of the truth', whilst 'meat' may refer to the 'clear revelation in the future world'. Reflecting on John 6:40, he writes:

> If, then, those who have believed have life, what remains beyond the possession of eternal life? Nothing is wanting to faith, as it is perfect and complete in itself. If aught is wanting to it, it is not wholly perfect. But faith is not lame in any respect; nor after our departure from this world does it make us who have believed, and received without distinction the earnest of future good, wait; but having in anticipation grasped by faith that which is future, after the resurrection we receive it as present, in order that that may be fulfilled which was spoken, "Be it according to thy faith".[5]

By 'earnest' ('pledge', Gk. *arrabōn*) he may be referring to the Holy Spirit (as in Ephesians 1:14). In his mind this saving faith is essentially linked with baptism for a little later he says, 'Instruction leads to faith, and faith with baptism is trained by the Holy Spirit. For that faith is the one universal salvation of humanity.' Everett Ferguson comments, 'Clement evidently saw no contradiction between affirming "faith alone" and affirming baptism as the occasion of initiation into essential spiritual blessings. Faith for him included baptism.'[6] Towards the end of *Instructor* 1.6 Clement quotes Philippians 3:12-14, noting that Paul does not think himself yet perfect. He concludes that in one sense perfection is achieved through the renunciation of sin, but yet there remains perfection in knowledge to which one must aspire.

In his later work *Miscellanies* we find Clement's thought has developed further.[7] He now says of 'milk' and 'meat' in 1 Corinthians 3:1-3: 'Milk' is catechetical instruction, 'the first food, as it were, of the soul', while 'meat' is 'the mystic contemplation; for this is the flesh and blood of the Word, that is, the comprehension of the divine power and essence' (*Miscellanies* 5.10). The bulk of *Miscellanies* is devoted to discussing and training the 'Gnostic', Clement's mature Christian who must achieve the total suppression of his passions. What

---

[5]   This and subsequent quotations from the works of Clement are from the Ante-Nicene Fathers II. 1885 (1995).

[6]   Everett Ferguson, *Baptism in the Early Church: history, theology and liturgy in the first five centuries* (Grand Rapids, MI: Eerdmans, 2009), p 314, n. 40.

[7]   So Einar Molland, *The Conception of the Gospel in Alexandrian Theology* (Oslo: Debured, 1938), p 78.

value now does he give to faith? In 1.7 he declares, 'Abraham was not justified by works, but by faith', commenting, 'It is therefore of no advantage (to Greek pagans) after the end of life, even if they do good works now, if they have not faith.' Again, in 2.6 he starts by quoting from Romans 10, noting particularly that 'faith comes by hearing, and hearing by the word of God' (v. 17), later saying, 'If to Abraham on his believing it was counted for righteousness; and if we are the seed of Abraham, then we must also believe through hearing' (Galatians 3:6-7). But, after further discussion he concludes, 'In truth, faith is discovered, by us, to be the first movement towards salvation; after which fear and hope, and repentance, advancing in company with temperance and patience, lead us to love and knowledge.' So now for him faith is a step into the wider field of Christian discipleship rather than, it seems, the vital means of attaining salvation.

In 5.1 he quotes Romans 1:17, 'The righteousness of God is revealed from faith to faith' deducing, 'The apostle, then, manifestly announces a two-fold faith, or rather one which admits of growth and perfection.' Now Paul's phrase 'from faith to faith' is probably no more than a rhetorical device emphasising the importance of faith,[8] but Clement finds in it support for his own emphasis on the need for *developing* faith. In 6.12 he returns to this idea, claiming support from the case of Abraham, 'On Abraham becoming a believer, it was reckoned to him for righteousness, he having advanced to the greater and more perfect degree of faith.' Clement's thought here is not clear but he seems to be saying that Abraham's actual step of trusting God's promise (Genesis 15:6) marked progress in his spiritual life.

When towards the end of *Instructor* 1.8 he has quoted Romans 3:21-22, 'But now the righteousness of God without the law is manifested...even the righteousness of God by the faith of Jesus Christ upon all who believe, for there is no difference', Clement then moves straight to vv.25b-26, 'through the forbearance of God, in order to show that He is just, and that Jesus is the justifier of him who is of faith'. His interest in this passage lies not in its statement about justification but merely in its value to prove, against heretics like Marcion, that one and the same God is just as well as good. His quotation omits Paul's key statement about the atonement in vv.24-25a. Perhaps we should not be surprised as Clement's references to Christ's death for our sins are so infrequent that many scholars have concluded Clement had no theology of the atonement at all. However Peter Ensor's recent study of

---

[8]   So Charles Harold Dodd, *The Epistle of Paul to the Romans* (London: Fontana Books, 1959), p 41.

Clement's writings has shown this view to be incorrect.9 He points out that Clement calls Christ 'the expiator (*katharsios*) of sin' (*Exhortation* 10), and speaks of Christians as filled with joy 'who have been redeemed from corruption by the blood of the Lord' (*Instructor* 1.5, cf. 1.6). He sometimes uses memorable metaphors for instance, in describing Christ's atoning work, he calls Christ a 'great cluster [of grapes], the Word, bruised for us' (*Instructor* 2.2), and 'the holy light which passed through from earth and returned again to heaven, by the wood [of the cross]...' (*Miscellanies* 1.24). In his sermon *Who is the Rich Man?* Clement says of God's love:

> For this also He came down. For this He clothed Himself with man. For this He voluntarily subjected Himself to the experiences of men, that by bringing Himself to the measure of our weakness whom He loved, He might correspondingly bring us to the measure of His own strength. And about to be offered up and giving Himself a ransom, He left for us a new Covenant... (37)

From these and other passages Ensor claims with some justice that Clement believed in Christ's substitutionary sacrifice for our sins, but he has to admit this does not hold a central place in Clement's thought.

There are in fact passages in which Clement clearly moves away from orthodoxy. In *Miscellanies* 6.9 he says it is ludicrous to think the Saviour ate to maintain the duration of his life, for his body was 'kept together by a holy energy'; furthermore, being entirely impassible, he was 'inaccessible to any movement of feeling – either pleasure or pain'. In *Miscellanies* 7.2 he says that the one we call Saviour and Lord...'Having assumed flesh, which by nature is susceptible of suffering, trained it to the condition of impassibility.' Later, telling how Jesus saves people, Clement says, 'Having assumed sensitive flesh, He came to show man what was possible through obedience to commandments.' The virtuous are attracted to him like particles of steel to a magnet. So here it appears Clement is saying people are saved by following Jesus' example. The *Miscellanies* are in fact devoted to training his Gnostic for just that: by faith, good works, and total suppression of his desires, eventually to achieve unbroken contemplation of God (as Moses had seen God face to face on Mount Horeb – *Miscellanies* 6.12). This is how he has come to understand perfection developed through

---

9   Peter Ensor, 'Clement of Alexandria and Penal Substitutionary Atonement', *Evangelical Quarterly* 85.1 (2013), pp 19-35.

knowledge. Here we find elements of Platonism[10] and Stoicism.[11] It seems then, by taking philosophy as an instructor, Clement has developed a considerably different understanding of Christianity from that of Paul.

---

[10] Cf. H. Chadwick, *Early Christian Thought and the Classical Tradition: Studies in Justin, Clement, and Origen* (Oxford: Clarendon Press, 1966), p 45; Vladimir Lossky, *The Vision of God*, 2nd edn (Leighton Buzzard: Faith Press, 1973), pp 41-2.

[11] Lossky, *Vision*, p 43.

Tertullian

Tertullian of Carthage, 'the father of Latin theology', was brought up a pagan. He was educated in rhetoric, philosophy and law, and was fluent in Greek as well as Latin. He appears to have been converted to Christ in middle life. From c.207 he came under the influence of Montanism, later separating himself from the mainstream Church which had rejected the Montanist prophets.[1] Nevertheless he remained orthodox in doctrine, producing in that period an admirable defence of the Trinity.[2] Thirty-one of his writings have been preserved, including important apologetic, catechetical and anti-heretical works. Jerome says that he was a presbyter,[3] but Tertullian denies that he was ordained.[4] Yet he writes with authority. It has been suggested he belonged to a North African Christian group of *seniores laici* ('lay elders').[5]

Like Clement, Tertullian believes in human freewill[6] and sees faith as rational choice in response to a carefully prepared presentation of the truth.[7] Whilst Tertullian is prepared to admit philosophers have sometimes alighted upon aspects of the truth, in contrast to Clement, he decries philosophy as the parent of heresy and of no value to the Christian.[8]

Tertullian accepts God's revelation in Scripture as the source of ultimate truth,[9] saying that usually one should take the literal meaning of its statements,[10] for he is well aware that heretics have often interpreted them perversely. He therefore, following Irenaeus, puts

---

[1] He referred to its members as the 'psychics' (the 'natural' as against the 'spiritual' Christians, 1 Corinthians 2:14) in contrast to those who recognized the genuineness of the Montanist prophets (*Against Praxeas* 1.2).

[2] *Against Praxeas* which, says Timothy D. Barnes, has won the greatest possible praise as 'a vigorous sketch of the Catholic position', *Tertullian: A Historical and Literary Study* (Oxford: University Press, 1971, 1985) p 142.

[3] Jerome, *Concerning Illustrious Men*, 53.

[4] *Exhortation to Chastity* 7.3, cf. *Monogamy* 12.1-4.

[5] David E. Wilhite in *Tertullian and Paul*, ed. Todd D. Still and David E. Wilhite, *Pauline and Patristic Scholars in Debate* I (New York: Bloomsbury, 2013) xix, alluding to the discussion of Gerald L. Bray, *Holiness and the Will of God* (London: Marshall, Morgan & Scott, 1979), pp 40-41.

[6] *On the Soul* 21, *Against Marcion* 2.4-7 et passim.

[7] Cf. Eric Osborn, *Tertullian, First Theologian of the West* (Cambridge: University Press, 1997), pp 46, 252-3.

[8] *Prescription against Heretics* 7.

[9] See Campenhausen, *Formation*, p 278.

[10] *Resurrection of the Flesh* 20.

forth the Church's 'rule of faith' (*regula fidei*) as a summary of Scripture and a clear guideline for its correct interpretation.[11] Though having as yet no fixed wording, the rule states the cardinal Christian beliefs about the three persons of the Godhead which later crystallized into the Apostles' Creed. Tertullian adhered to it to the end, and so, even in his strongly Montanist days, he could write:

> We... believe... that the one only God has also a Son, his Word who has proceeded from himself, by whom all things were made and without whom nothing has been made: that this (Son) was sent by the Father into the virgin and was born of her both man and God, Son of man and Son of God, and was named Jesus Christ: that he suffered, died, and was buried, according to the scriptures, and, having been raised up by the Father and taken back into heaven, sits at the right hand of the Father and will come to judge the quick[12] and the dead: and that thereafter he, according to his promise, sent from the Father the Holy Spirit the Paraclete, the sanctifier of the faith of those who believe in the Father and the Son and the Holy Spirit. (*Against Praxeas* 2, tr. Evans)

And he declares that the rule had come down from the 'beginning of the Gospel', i.e. from the apostles.[13] Although he could sarcastically refer to Paul as 'the apostle of the heretics',[14] in reality for Tertullian Paul is 'the Apostle'[15] and he repeatedly quotes him, clearly regarding him as authoritative on matters of faith and practice, sometimes mentioning which epistle he is quoting from.[16] In his longest work, the masterly *Against Marcion*, in his exposition of Galatians (and more briefly Romans) Tertullian sets down without disparagement Paul's doctrine of justification by faith. In 5.2.1 he declares that Galatians is the primary epistle against Judaism, commenting 'we receive with open arms all that abolition of the ancient law'.[17] But, against Marcion, he needs to

---

[11] *Prescription against Heresies* 19.2-3. Bray points out that Tertullian here follows contemporary Roman understanding of the word *regula* which was not just a measure of straightness but also prescriptive: 'The *regula fidei* was a summary of the *lex* (i.e. Scripture) which could then be used as a fundamental rule in biblical interpretation', *Holiness*, p 103.

[12] Latin: *vivos*, 'living'.

[13] Cf. *Prescription against Heresies* 37.

[14] *Against Marcion* 3.5.4.

[15] *On Prayer* 20.1, *On Baptism* 17.2 et passim

[16] E.g. *Prescription against Heresies* 4-6, *Monogamy* 10-14. His interpretations are not always legitimate. The recent symposium between Patristic and Pauline scholars *Tertullian and Paul*, ed. Still and Wilhite fascinatingly explores a number of facets of this subject.

[17] Though in fact he makes very little use of it in his early work *Against the Jews*.

stress that the God who gave the law is the same God who has given the pathway of faith in Christ, fulfilling Old Testament prophecy (which Marcion dismisses as worthless). Commenting on Galatians 2:16 (and Psalm 2:3 and Habakkuk 2:4) he says:

> Let the apostle proceed with his statement that by the works of the law a man is not justified, but only by faith. The faith however is of that same God whose also is the law... Now a man is justified by the freedom of faith and not by the bondage of the law: because the just liveth by faith: and as the prophet Habakkuk said this first, you have also the apostle expressing agreement with the prophets, as Christ himself did. (*Against Marcion* 5.3.8-9, Evans)

Marcion has erased Paul's reference to Abraham[18] from his copy of Galatians but still retained the statement 'you are all sons of faith', so Tertullian enquires, what then is meant by 'sons of faith'? And he supplies the answer: if Abraham believed God and it was reckoned for righteousness, we by believing God are justified and obtain life, and so we are sons of Abraham (5.3.11-12).

Later, in connection with Romans 5:1, Tertullian says, 'Of old there was the law, but now the righteousness of God by the faith of Christ (*per fidem Christi*)... He enjoins us who are justified, not by law but by the faith of Christ (*ex fide Christi, non ex lege*) to have peace towards God' (5.13.8-9). Evans here translates the Latin literally. But Tertullian does not spell out that he is referring to Christ's own faith or faithfulness in dying on the cross to redeem sinful mankind, he merely reiterates that it is the same God to whom belong the law and 'the faith of Christ'. He does not then necessarily lend support here to the 'new perspective'. He is merely contrasting the two courses of divine action, the first in providing the law, the second in sending Christ in whom people should believe. Peter Holmes translates 5.13.9, 'He enjoins those who are justified by faith in Christ, and not by the law to have peace with God' (Ante-Nicene Fathers).

Whilst Tertullian does not state in these passages on justification by faith that he believes the subject of a Christian's faith should be the atoning sacrifice of Christ, it is clear from a number of other passages that this is so. In *Flesh of Christ* 4 he speaks of Christ's death on the cross as due to his love for man, for 'he redeemed him at a great price'. In *Flight in Persecution* 12 Tertullian deplores the suggestion that a Christian might pay money to escape persecution. How unworthy it would be, he says, to ransom with money one whom Christ ransomed

---

[18]   Being from the Old Testament.

with his blood! God did not spare his Son but made him a curse for us when he was hanged on a tree. Christ was led like a sheep to be a sacrifice for us. All this to redeem us from our sins. In *Against Marcion* 3.8 Tertullian berates Marcion for his Docetism: if Christ was not really human, he says, neither was his suffering real and the Gospel of salvation (he quotes 1 Corinthians 15:3-4) is subverted.

There remains one further matter to consider. One might so emphasise the vital importance of faith that baptism appears redundant. In his work *On Baptism* Tertullian declares some miscreants have taken this line, pointing to Abraham who pleased God by faith alone (13.1). He is aware that one might add that the twelve apostles were not baptised by Christ, but thinks their case was exceptional (12). But for subsequent Christians he declares:

> Let us suppose that formerly, before our Lord's passion and resurrection, salvation was by faith unattired: yet now that the faith has been enlarged, for those who believe in his nativity and passion and resurrection, the sacrament has been expanded and the seal of baptism added, in some sense a clothing for the faith which was previously unattired: and (faith) can no longer save apart from its own law. For there has been imposed a law of baptizing and its form prescribed: Go, he says, teach the nations, baptizing them in the Name of the Father and the Son and the Holy Ghost. When this law was associated with that pronouncement Except a man have been born again of water and the Holy Spirit he shall not enter into the kingdom of heaven, faith was put under obligation to the necessity of baptism. Consequently from then onwards all believers began to be baptized. (13.2-3, Evans)

And he points to the case of Paul (Acts 9). In this, the first surviving treatise on baptism, Tertullian clearly articulates the Church's normative position. But is this position not in reality close to that of Paul who says to the Galatians, 'In Christ Jesus you are all children of God through faith. As many of you as were baptized into Christ have clothed yourselves with Christ' (Galatians 3:26-7)?

In Conclusion

Daniel Williams, whose article we cited at the beginning of this paper, said that the doctrine of justification by faith was not noticed before Origen (c.185-c.254) in the East and Hilary (c.315-c.254) in the West. Well, this doctrine may not have been seriously discussed before these writers, but it was certainly noticed. All six writers that we have studied mention justification, echoing or quoting Paul's actual words. But Paul's battle to establish his Gospel against opposition from the Judaizers was over. By the second century Gentiles formed the majority of the Church and they were not required to keep the Jewish Law. So of what value was justification?

As we have seen, in chapter 32.4 of his epistle Clement of Rome quoted this doctrine. Confronted with arrogant, young men who had risen up and deposed the duly elected elders of the Corinthian church, Clement pointed out that Christians are justified by faith not their own works. He uses this as an argument for humility. But he goes on to insist that this doctrine does not excuse Christians from devoting themselves to good works. Dodson rightly observes of the writers of the second century in general, since all people saved by faith must live moral lives, 'more stress was placed on the necessity of righteous living than on the doctrine of salvation alone'.[1]

The case of Ignatius is rather different. Writing his letters hurriedly on a forced march from Antioch to martyrdom in Rome he has little time for reflection or making exact quotations, but his references to Jesus' death saving us from death and judgment and his use of the term 'justify' in connection with Jesus' death, resurrection and faith suggest he knows Romans or Galatians and is aware of their cardinal doctrine. But for reasons we can only guess, he is passionately concerned to go to a martyr's death in Rome in imitation of Paul and Jesus himself, and his assurance of salvation appears to depend on doing so.

Justin does not mention Paul. We have discussed possible reasons for this. But many would agree that in his *Dialogue with Trypho a Jew* he echoes several times Paul's statement that Christians like Abraham are justified before God by faith, and he also appears familiar with Paul's argument in Galatians 3 that Christ, by being 'hanged on a tree', took upon himself the curse of the law. Despite his philosophical training and insights Justin shows himself a true servant of the Gospel.

---

[1]   Bird & Dodson, *Paul*, p 3.

Irenaeus, undoubtedly the greatest Christian theologian of the second century, has no doubts about the legitimacy of Paul as an apostle and readily speaks of justification by faith. He sees it as a fruit of recapitulation, his favourite concept for explaining how Christ achieved salvation for humankind. This concept is surely a legitimate elaboration of statements of Paul himself. It is unfair to accuse him of pedalling 'another gospel'.

Clement of Alexandria was, like Justin, a converted philosopher. To him faith in Christ is important for attaining salvation, but his great concern is to move Christians on from simple faith to maturity, with the ultimate goal of permanent contemplation of the face of God. It is a noble aim, but while he sees philosophy of continuing importance in this endeavour, he seems to lose sight of justification by faith. He thus takes a different path from that of Paul, but it was one followed by later influential Greek Fathers and has had a permanent influence on Orthodox spirituality. It is unfortunate that Clement used the name 'gnostic' for his mature Christian for that name is indelibly associated with heretics of the second century and later. While his emphasis on progress in the spiritual life and self-control are fine, his desire to eliminate a person's desires would seem to have more in common with Buddhism than biblical Christianity.

Tertullian desired to be biblical and shunned philosophy as the parent of heresy. He frequently quoted the writings of Paul, including on occasion the doctrine of justification by faith. In one of his early writings he declares forcefully that Christian faith must be sealed by baptism. Latterly, despite falling out of fellowship with the mainline Church for its rejection of Montanism, which he believed embodied true charismatic spirituality and asceticism, he appears to have remained faithful to the essential doctrines of the Church as shown in his ability to articulate clearly its Rule of Faith.

Dodson says that second-century writers 'manipulated the meaning and appealed to the value of Paul to support their own arguments and to treat new ideas in new situations'. Is that true of justification? To some extent it is. Clement of Rome fairly appealed to this doctrine to urge humility upon the Corinthian church, but Clement of Alexandria read into Paul's statement that 'the righteousness of God is revealed from faith to faith' endorsement of his own concern for 'growth and perfection' in the Christian life. Other examples could be cited. But in the main, it would seem, our writers quoted Paul's doctrine without distorting it. When it was not relevant to their concerns they did not mention it.

Do we find any trace of the modern debate as to whether *pistis Christou* is a 'subjective' or 'objective' genitive in the writings we have studied? No, but our English translators show some uncertainty. In the Ante-Nicene Fathers translation of Clement of Alexandria's *Instructor* 1.8 the phrase is rendered 'faith of Christ' (a subjective genitive). Ernest Evans translates the Latin equivalent *fidem/fide Christi* in Tertullian's *Against Marcion* 5.13.8-9 similarly, but in the Ante-Nicene Fathers version it is once translated 'faith in Christ' (an 'objective' genitive). In neither passage did the Father concerned make any comment on this phrase. His concern lay elsewhere. This matter would benefit from an in-depth study far beyond the scope of this paper. Perhaps uncertainty as to the correct meaning of the phrase contributed to the Fathers' reticence to quote it!

And what is there of practical value for us in this study? The fact that the Fathers continued to speak about justification surely indicates its enduring value. In the words of a much later writer, 'That we are justified by faith only, is a most wholesome doctrine, and very full of comfort' (*Articles of Religion*, No. 11). It saves us from tormenting fear that our lives may not be good enough to ensure for us a place in heaven. But, Clement of Rome reminds us, it should make us humble, for we have not by our merits earned salvation. And we should devote ourselves to good works in gratitude. Further, Tertullian is right to insist that our faith should be sealed by baptism, for being a Christian is not just a private affair, we are part of the community of believers, the Church. And from the moment of baptism (and here Clement of Alexander is right), all Christians should seek to grow spiritually and practice self-discipline for we are preparing for that day when we shall see our Lord face to face (1 John 3:2-3).

Justification is only one of the metaphors Paul uses for Christ's work of salvation. It comes from the law courts (declaring in the right, acquittal); he speaks also of 'reconciliation' (2 Corinthians 5:18-21) from the field of human relationships, 'redemption' (Romans 3:24), a metaphor from the slave market, and 'sacrifice' (Ephesians 5:2), from the life of the temple. Sometimes he simply emphasizes salvation is a matter of God's grace (Ephesians 2:8, Titus 3:7). Other metaphors were used by later writers, such as Irenaeus' notion 'recapitulation' (derived ultimately from Paul), and the picture of Jesus Christ as a 'peace child', from a ritual used to bring peace between warring, head-hunting tribes in New Guinea.[2] There must be many other examples as the Christian faith has penetrated new cultures throughout the world during its two-thousand year history.

---

[2]   The story is movingly told by Don Richardson in his book *Peace Child*, now in its 4th ed. (Ventura, CA: Regal Books, 2005).

If you have enjoyed this book, you might like to consider

- *supporting the work of the Latimer Trust*
- *reading more of our publications*
- *recommending them to others*

See www.latimertrust.org for more information.

Latimer Publications

Lightning Source UK Ltd.
Milton Keynes UK
UKOW04f2134030415

249064UK00002B/47/P